MW01611596

GOVERNED BY LOVE

The New Law for the New You

GOVERNED BY LOVE

The New Law for the New You

JEFFREY R.GLOVER

My motivation for writing this book is to counter a prophetic word given in the book of Matthew 24:12 that the love of many shall wax cold because of iniquity. As I began to study and research the text I noticed it was referencing agapé love that only Believers carry!

You see, although it was a prophetic word and it will come to pass, this book is written to provide the remnant with a detailed understanding of the power, depth, and intended purpose of being carriers of God's love. Too many marriages are failing and friendships deteriorating because we have yet to distinguish the difference between the love we were naturally born with and the love we inherited from God. This book is the beginning of many that will provide comprehensive insight on the power of God's love like never before!

The love of God has totally revolutionized my life, and as you read each chapter you will experience the miracle for yourself!

Gloria, I cannot thank you enough for your undying support, encouraging words, and the strength that you add to the relationship!

I thank you for your unwavering resolve and belief in me. You have demonstrated your love for me many times over as you follow me as I follow Christ; for that I dedicate this work to you.

Contents

Acknowledgements

To family: I sincerely thank my parents, Rudy and Florence Glover (Dad & Mom) who have always been a great support and inspiration to me. Thank you for your experience, wisdom, unconditional love, and support that you have always given to me.

Spiritual Dad & Mom Dr. Creflo and Taffi Dollar: I thank you so much for the spiritual upbringing that has prepared me to fulfill the call of God on my life. It is through your impartation that I was filled with the passion to thoroughly explore the topic of love. I look forward to many more years of impartation through CDMA conferences.

Church Family: I sincerely thank the faithful, dedicated, steadfast, and loyal members of Perfecting the Saints Church International who have been there and will be there until the fulfillment of the vision.

Book Editor (Suzanne Daniels): I sincerely thank you for your diligence, dedication, and attention to detail.

Vision Partners: I sincerely thank all of our Vision Partners of Perfecting the Saints Church International in the city of San Antonio, Texas and Atlanta, Georgia. Your continual support enables us to touch the lives of those near and far. Every life that is touched through media, books, CDs, and DVDs will go toward your account. Stay in expectation of a great harvest!

Introduction

When it comes to being transformed into the image of God in our character, there is a very specific role we play in achieving this goal. The Word of God exhorts Believers to get rid of their old ways of doing things and embrace God's method of operation. One thing we must realize is that when we become born again we become new creatures in Christ. Our spirits are instantly made new and we now have the potential to act, think, and speak just like God! However, in order to actually see this come to pass in our lives, we must allow the Holy Spirit to transform us in our souls, which includes the mind, will, and emotions.

The process of salvation is 3-fold. It involves the rebirth of a man's spirit, the regeneration of the soul, and ultimately the resurrection of the body. The first part is completed when we accept Jesus into our hearts, but the regeneration of the soul requires work on our part. We must make it a point to renew our minds on a daily basis in order to align our thinking with God's Word.

The restoration of the soul compartment is necessary because it is the part of us that ultimately determines where we spend eternity. When Adam sinned in the Garden of Eden and ate of the Tree of the Knowledge of Good and Evil, he severed his connection with God, not only in his spirit, but also in his soul. In fact, his act of high treason caused his mind, will, and emotions to become contaminated with sin. His disobedience left him with a fragmented soul that was vulnerable to the input of the enemy.

The good news is that when we become born again we inherit the love of God. This love is intended to not only restore and heal our damaged souls, but to govern us from the inside out. Love is a law that, when activated, will revolutionize our lives.

FIRST THINGS FIRST

"Jesus said unto him, thou shalt love the Lord thy God with all thy heart, and with all thy soul, and with all thy mind." (Matthew 22:37)

As we go about our daily routines, it is easy to become caught up in the busyness of life. Trying to secure our basic needs can be an exhausting task when our priorities are out of order. Whether we realize it or not, God has established specific guidelines and priorities by which we are to live. As Christians, adhering to these guidelines is our responsibility.

The order God has established is as follows: God first, family second, and ministry/church responsibilities third. Whenever we become so busy that this order is disrupted, we will find ourselves struggling unnecessarily on so many levels. God never intended for us to have to struggle or toil in life, but when our priorities are out of line, we will experience difficulties in areas that should be sweatless.

The truth is, things get out of sequence when we don't have a true revelation of what our top priority should be—maintaining our relationship with God. When we possess an in-depth knowledge of God's existence,

...u iiow He longs to be in fellowship with us, our relationship with Him will dramatically improve. Keeping first things first has everything to do with the measure of love we have for Him and the intimate knowledge we have of who He really is.

When it comes to knowing God, our knowledge of Him must exceed mental assent, or "head" knowledge, and move to the place where it becomes "heart" knowledge. Many Believers short change their relationship with the Lord by trying to jump to His blessings and supernatural manifestations without cultivating a genuine relationship with Him. This simply doesn't work! If we do not have a personal relationship with God for ourselves, all we really have is religion. God wants much more.

John 4:24 says, *"God is a Spirit: and they that worship Him must worship Him in spirit and in truth."* This passage really hones in on the type of transparency and genuineness God is looking for in our relationship with Him. First, we cannot even begin to know God unless we are in the spirit, which essentially means to abide in His Word and make it our final authority. Remaining connected to His Word will give us true heart knowledge of who He is. When we become one with His Word, we will have utmost confidence that greater is He that is in us than he that is in the world. We will be convinced we can do all things through Christ.

Falling in Love with God

Loving God is the way we keep Him first in our lives. In fact, we cannot reasonably say we are keeping first things first if we are not in love with the Lord. When we love Him, we will want to please Him in everything we do, including our daily decisions.

Matthew 22:37 gives the love commandments which we are to abide by as Christians. It says, *"Jesus said unto him, thou shalt love the Lord thy God with all thy heart, and with all thy soul, and with all thy mind."* When Jesus speaks about loving God with our hearts, He is referring to the spirit of man; the place where the Holy Spirit dwells. To love Him with the soul, which includes the mind, will, and emotions, means to love Him with our faculties and understanding. Truly loving God requires a total commitment to the relationship.

As Believers, our first order of business is to love God with all of our being. As we fall in love with Him we will find a level of intimacy being established that will elevate our knowledge and awareness of who He really is.

I have come to realize that most people have a superficial relationship with God rather than one of quality and personal experience. However, when we make a commitment to our relationship with Him, we won't have a problem serving Him wholeheartedly and disobedience will diminish. We will want to give Him our best at all times.

Knowing Him For Real

Wouldn't you agree that it is nearly impossible to have a relationship with someone you barely know, or with someone who will not allow you to go beyond a surface level of interaction? The same is true with how we relate to our Creator. Many Believers fall short in certain areas of their lives because they don't have a working revelation of who He really is and they never get to the place of real intimacy with Him. When we really know God, it will bring us into a realm of awe and reverence that compels us to be obedient, further demonstrating our love for Him.

Knowing God ties back in to His Word, which tells us everything we need to know about His character and way of doing things. The more time we spend studying and meditating on the Word of God, the more we get a picture of who God is. As we discover new and exciting things about Him, the relationship we have with Him will develop.

Hebrews 11:6 describes some interesting things about knowing God and pleasing Him. It says, *"But without faith it is impossible to please Him: for he that cometh to God must believe that He is, and that He is a rewarder of them that diligently seek Him."*

This passage clearly communicates that we must have faith in order to please God. In addition, anyone who comes to Him must fulfill the prerequisite of believing that He exists! This is the first step to knowing Him. When we believe in His existence, it will boost our confidence in Him and what He is able to do. We won't have a problem believing His Word and acting on it without hesitation. We must grasp the true reality of His existence.

When we believe He is real, we must then put Him in the top priority spot in our lives. The account of Mary and Martha in Luke 10:38-40 describes how important this is:

> *"Now it came to pass, as they went, that he entered into a certain village; and a certain woman named Martha received Him into her house. And she had a sister called Mary, which also sat at Jesus' feet, and heard His word. But Martha was cumbered about much serving, and came to Him, and said, Lord, dost thou not care that my sister hath left me to serve alone? Bid her that she therefore help me. And Jesus answered and said unto her, Martha, Martha, thou art careful and troubled about many*

things: But one thing is needful: and Mary hath
Chosen that good part, which shall not be taken
away from her."

Martha thought the top priority should be to wait on the Lord and serve Him. This could be equated to being overly concerned with the outward acts of religion. However, Jesus clarified that her outward busyness interfered with her choosing what she needed most—sitting at His feet and partaking of His presence. I am sure if Martha had done this, she would have gleaned valuable insight that would have only enhanced her ability to serve God even more effectively.

Do you find yourself spending more time doing "things" than you do spending time in the presence of God? If so, it is time to make an adjustment. You won't be able to serve Him properly if you don't know Him personally. Keeping first things first means giving God time and attention before anything else. This is the path to true and lasting peace. When we do this, He will reveal Himself to us in ways we never imagined.

I like what Psalm 73:25 says, *"Whom have I in the earth but thee? And there is none upon the earth that I desire besides thee."* Simply put, there can be no one and nothing that has higher precedence than God in our lives. God longs for His creation to return to fellowship with Him; He wants relationship with us! Spending time with Him regularly will open us up to who He really is.

Whether you realize it or not, God is always knocking on the door of our hearts, in an attempt to draw us closer to Him. He loves us so much that He will never stop trying to get our attention. Whether we answer the door or not is up to us. Nevertheless, He will remain faithful to continue knocking. He is willing to wait until we come to the door, only because He knows we are inside the house!

I want to encourage you to make a quality decision to develop a quality relationship with God and get to know Him on a more personal level. Putting first things first will not only dramatically enhance your relationship with Him, but it will make your life a whole lot sweeter. Dare to make Him top priority and watch Him invade your life with unprecedented blessings. It's a guarantee!

2

GOVERNED BY LOVE

"I will put my law in their inward parts, and write it in their hearts…" **(Jeremiah 31:33)**

As we begin to study the Word of God, there are so many exciting things He will reveal to us. I like to call them "jewels of wisdom." These nuggets of truth are the treasures our heavenly Father has hidden for those who diligently seek Him. One of the most important revelations I have discovered as I continue to search the Scriptures is the revelation of the love of God. Understanding God's precious gift of love and learning how to activate it in our lives is the most valuable thing we can do as Believers.

The message of love is one that is not always preached with the fervor and intensity as other subjects in the Bible. However, I have come to realize that in order for us to truly exemplify the character and image of God, love must become the force that governs our lives from the inside out.

Where It All Began

God is love and everything He does is based on love. I want to revisit Genesis 1:26, where God first created mankind: *"And God said, Let us make man in our image and after our likeness…"* Clearly, He originally intended for us to represent Him in the Earth. We were created just like Him in that we are spiritual beings who possess creative power and the ability to love the way He does.

You see, God wanted us to possess His characteristics, which is why He patterned man after Himself. Adam was created to have dominion in the Earth. He was equipped with every resource he needed to carry out God's will.

One way to look at it is that God "uploaded" all the necessary programs on Adam's "hard drive" in order for him to live up to God's original expectation. However, when Adam ate the fruit of the Tree of Knowledge of Good and Evil, his spiritual "hard drive" became infected by the enemy.

Fortunately, there is an antidote to the "viruses" that infected man's spirit in the Garden. It is the love of God! When love is allowed to dominate us, we default to the original purpose for which He created us. The love of God is the root to the power and dominion in which we are to walk.

Governed by Love

To *govern* means "to control, direct, rule, determine, and restrain." As it relates to Christians, we are to be controlled, directed, ruled, and restrained by love in order to walk as sons of God in the earth. Remember God said "let us make man in our image…" God's image is love, and when we conform our lives to that standard, we will be able to execute the authority He has given us. However, until we fully yield our spirits, souls, and bodies to God, Who is love, we will never know or experience His fullness in our lives.

In order to walk in His image we must be convinced of who we are. I like what First John 4:7, 8 says:

> *"Beloved, let us love one another: for love is of God; and every one that Loveth is born of God, and knoweth God. He that loveth not knoweth not God; for God is Love."*

Love is what makes God "God" and if we are to be like Him, we must walk in love as well. We must know we were made as exact spiritual replicas of the Father. If God is love and we are born of God, than we must also be love. In fact, love was a part of our original makeup. Love is not only what we have, it is who we are. When we allow ourselves to be governed by love it will restore broken relationships and bring healing to our nation. Once we are convinced of our identities, nothing and no one will be able to rob us of what God has promised us.

The Love Deposit Has Been Made

Did you know the same love God has for mankind has been deposited in your heart? That's right! The very same love God possesses is residing in the heart of every Christian. It is simply up to you to draw it out.

Romans 5:5 says, "*And hope maketh not ashamed; because the love of God is shed abroad in our hearts by the Holy Ghost which is given unto us.*" The love of God in you is similar to an egg that has not yet hatched. Imagine the Holy Spirit roosting on that egg. Right now the love of God in you may still be in a shell, but the more you cultivate it, a piece of the shell will fall away. Every time you walk in love and act in love, more pieces of shell will fall away until, one day, you will discover the fullness of God's love invading every fiber of your being, ultimately transforming you completely into His image. This is what it means to truly be *governed* by the love of God.

Please understand that who we are in this natural, earthly realm doesn't make us who we are in the spirit. However, who we are from a spiritual perspective influences and determines our lives in this natural world. It is a life controlled by love that gives us access to God's power.

Love Takes Control

Too often, our true nature—love—has been hidden by past hurts and negative experiences. But even so, we must begin to reconnect with the essence of who we are as Believers. Love adds equity to our character. The devil has been trying to keep this from us for years because he knows that when we get a true revelation of God's love, we become a great threat to his kingdom. Not only that but it will enable us to operate on a higher level of life. Love is an eternal, everlasting force that is limitless in its working and power. It is our true identity.

When we identify with love, it will even begin to affect the way we speak. The eyes of our understanding will be opened, and we will be quickened from the inside before we say or do anything contrary to the Word of God. When we become controlled by love, the love of God in us now becomes the inward law.

The area of speech is a critical one because our words literally create things in our lives. James 3:4 says, *"Behold also the ships, which though they be so great, and are driven of fierce winds, yet are they turned about with a very small helm, whithersoever the governor listeth."* This passage, which draws an analogy between the tongue (mouth) and the helm of a ship, shows how the words we speak have the potential to direct our lives on a certain course.

The Word tells us that our mouths speak based on the abundance of what is in our hearts. If our hearts are governed by love, we will be more mindful of what comes out of our mouths. And when our words are in line with love, our actions will follow suit. We will find it difficult to strive against one another or use our words to hurt or wound others.

James 3:2 says, *"For in many things we offend all. If any man offend not in word, the same is a perfect man, and able also to bridle the whole body."* How we communicate with our words makes the difference when it comes to avoiding offense. Even during times when a serious conversation is necessary, we must always employ love in our approach.

Our primary objective is to ensure the seed of understanding is deposited in the other person's heart. Everything from our tone of voice, facial expressions, and body language sends a message. If we are angry, hostile, and bitter, our listeners will shut down on us and won't be able to receive what we have to say. We must make sure our personal motives are to truly communicate our perspective in love, and we also want to make sure that what we want to talk about is truly a Kingdom issue and not a petty concern that is birthed out of personal insecurities.

Always remember the love of God is what purifies our hearts and keeps our motives in check at all times. Choosing the proper timing and place to communicate are also indicative of walking in the love of God so as not to unnecessarily provoke a person to offense.

When we relinquish control of our lives to God, love will become the guardian of our minds *and* our mouths. The more conscious we become of God's nature within us, we will find ourselves becoming better custodians over our thoughts and words. Those things that do not please Him will get checked at the door! Love will take control when we give ourselves over to it (2 Corinthians 5:14, *The Amplified Bible*).

Love Fulfills the Law

Many of us are familiar with the Ten Commandments, and there are those who look at the Old Testament law as the standard by which we are to live our lives. However, the New Covenant of love, ratified with the blood of Jesus, is preeminent because it actually *fulfills* everything set forth in the Old Testament. In Matthew 5:17, Jesus said, *"Think not that I am come to destroy the law, or the prophets: I am not come to destroy, but to fulfil."* To *fulfill* means "to completely fill, cover, or make level."

Have you ever had the awful experience of driving over a pothole in the street? That pothole causes your ride to be bumpy and uncomfortable. In fact, it can make driving a complete hassle and can ruin your tires. This is how the law of the Old Testament could be viewed. It actually tripped people up, in a sense, because of their sins. The old law of old was literally established as an external governor of people's lives to deter them from disobeying God. Unfortunately, because Jesus had not yet come on the scene, man was not redeemed from sin. The people at that time had to constantly make sacrifices to atone for the times they broke the law.

However, when Jesus showed up He fulfilled the law through one dynamic principle—love. It is our love for God that compels us to want to obey Him. When we love God and others, we automatically fulfill the laws He originally set forth. Love is the great equalizer.

Jeremiah 31:33 talks about the new covenant:

> *"But this shall be the covenant that I make with the house of Israel; After those days, saith the Lord, I will put my law in their inward parts, and write it in their hearts; and will be their God, and they shall be my people."*

What is God saying here? He is saying that only when we allow the inward law, which is love, to govern us from the inside out, will we begin to know Him personally. Not only that, but we will automatically fulfill all external laws. He wants us to experience Him in a much more intimate way and love is the gateway to that type of relationship with the Father.

First Corinthians 13:4-8 (AMP) describes the characteristics of love that every Believer should strive to embrace:

> *"Love endures long and is patient and kind; love never is envious nor boils over with jealousy, is not boastful or vainglorious, does not display itself haughtily. It is not conceited (arrogant and inflated with pride); it is not rude (unmannerly) and does not act unbecomingly. Love (God's love in us) does not insist on its own rights or its own way, for it is not self seeking; it is not touchy or fretful or resentful; it takes no account to evil done to it [it pays no attention to a suffered wrong]. It does not rejoice at injustice and unrighteousness, but rejoices when right and truth prevail. Love bears up under anything and everything that comes, is ever ready to believe the best of every person, its hopes are fadeless under all circumstances, and endures everything*

[without weakening]. Love never fails [never fades out or becomes obsolete or comes to an end]..."

When we really begin to look at this description of love, we have no choice but to conduct a personal evaluation of our own love walk. We must ask ourselves if our words, actions, conduct, and character measure up to the standard set forth in the Word. If not, we have the ability to make the necessary adjustments.

I love 1 Corinthians 13 because it really encapsulates the major issues that can interfere with us having and maintaining successful relationships. This chapter is the guideline for how to walk in love. As we allow the love of God to govern us, it will get rid of the selfishness, envy, offense, and pride that destroy relationships, and even society as a whole.

We have the power to make a difference by allowing the character of God to become the dominating force in our lives. Although there are many members of the body of Christ, there is one unique and eternal thread that connects us to one another—the love of God. Allow it to govern your life so you can be an accurate representation of Jesus Christ wherever you go!

SIN'S ANTIDOTE

"He that loveth not knoweth not God; for God is Love." (1 John 4:8)

"...whosoever abides in Him sinneth not...." (1 John 3:6-10)

It is no secret that sin is an ongoing problem that has been haunting the lives of too many Christians. I purposely used the word *haunting* because according to the Word of God sin has actually been nullified in the life of a Believer, by the power of the blood of Jesus. It has no real power except what we supply it through our own lust.

What is sin? It can be looked at as spiritual poison that entered into our bloodline through Adam. It is a part of our fallen, carnal nature, which compels us to do things that go against the Word of God. Thankfully, God has supplied us with His love, which is the antidote that reverses the process of sin in our lives.

An *antidote* is a remedy or cure which counteracts the effects of a poison. We know very well the story of Adam and Eve's fall in the Garden of Eden. Genesis 3:6 gives the account of Adam and Eve eating of the forbidden fruit. As soon as Adam bit the fruit, he ingested a poison that was so deadly that death began a courtship with mankind, thus altering his original makeup. As soon as they ate the fruit this spiritual poison, in the form of a curse, invaded their spirits, souls, and bodies and they immediately entered into the death process. We have to keep in mind that God told Adam, "**In the day** that you eat of the tree thou shalt surely die." Although Adam lived 930 years, due to the spiritual principle of one day being equated to a thousand years to the Lord, Adam did not even finish out the day! Sin had infected man, and it not only affected his physical body and life span, but it now began to govern his thought life and every action.

All of us were bound to the lifestyle of sin and death with no hope of escape until the love of God reached out to mankind in the form of a man named Jesus. Two thousand years ago, on the cross of Calvary, a special sacrifice was made for our sins by our Lord and Savior, Jesus Christ. Through Adam, sin entered the world, but through Jesus, we have all been made righteous through the free gift of salvation (Romans 5:12-15). God's grace is overflowing and His love for mankind is endless!

So we see, according to the Word of God, that sin is no longer the Believer's problem; it has been taken care of by the blood of Jesus Christ. However, it is the unrenewed mind that continues to compel us to sin. This is why it is so important that we renew our minds with God's Word.

Sin never starts out as an act; there is a process involved and it looks like this: first the enemy presents a temptation which comes in the form of a thought or suggestion that appeals to one of your five senses. If left unchecked, that thought will then invade your mind and become lust, which is a strong appetite for whatever you gave your attention to. Once lust is fully developed, the desire will be so intense that it compels you to sin. Sin's ultimate result is death, or separation from God, spiritually and physically.

The only way for sin to truly have dominion in our lives is if we abide in the flesh, which is a way of thinking that opposes the Word of God. First Corinthians 15:34 says, "*Awake to righteousness, and sin not.*" This simply means that sin is a matter of choice. When Jesus died for us, He empowered those who believe and receive Him as their Lord and Savior to overcome sin. When we allow the inward law of love to govern our lives, it compels us and motivates us to change (Romans 2:4).

To get a clear view of how love empowers us to be victorious over sin, we can insert the word "love" in the scriptures where God is mentioned. For example, if we apply this to 1 John 5:3, 4 it would read this way, *"For this is the love of God, that we keep His commandments: and His commandments are not grievous. So whatsoever is born of **love** overcometh the world: and this is the victory that overcometh the world, even our faith."* Verses 3-4 clearly communicate that the love of God is what enables us to keep His commandments. When love is abounding in us it energizes our faith and enables us to overcome the temptations the enemy throws our way. When we are born of love, we turn away from our old commitment to sin, making us inaccessible to the enemy. When we receive Jesus in our hearts we receive the byproducts of love, which include healing, prosperity, and long, strong life!

The key to staying out of sin is to abide in love (1 John 3:6-10). You cannot live in two places simultaneously; it is one or the other. So likewise, when you continually dwell in love, you are not abiding in sin and you demonstrate that you are God's offspring. This love is what empowers and infuses us with life, regenerating our spirits, and purifying our hearts. The more we cultivate love we will find it flushing out the residue of sin, leaving us free to live the life God planned for us.

THE MORE YOU LOVE, THE LONGER YOU LIVE

"He taught me also, and said unto me, let thine heart retain my words: keep my commandments and live."
(Proverbs 4:4)

One of the primary objectives of this book is to reveal the unlimited capability of God's love, and show how that love has the potential to absolutely revolutionize our lives. Love is the catalyst to wisdom, peace, joy, and power; it amplifies the effectiveness of our spiritual gifts. Not only that, but living a life that is governed by love brings longevity and improves the quality of life. It is just that powerful.

Most people desire to live a long time and even spend a lot of money in an attempt to prolong their lives. Unfortunately, many do not see their golden years. Sickness, disease, and the results of sin claim the lives of people every day. There are numerous reasons why people may die early, but the truth remains that it is definitely God's will for us to live long, strong lives that glorify Him in every way. While it is critical that we maintain good health to the best of our ability by getting exercise, proper nutrition, and sufficient rest, there is a missing link that is even more crucial to obtaining long life—the unseen force of God's love working in us. Developing this love will bring about longevity.

The Thread that Connects Us

Love is more than just a vague concept or a cute word we throw around on Valentine's Day! I am convinced that it is the sustainer of our natural and spiritual lives, and that it even triggers healing agents in our bodies that ward off disease. It is the divine thread of God's essence and life that connects us all.

Many times in the medical field, it is concluded that the elderly die of old age. However, from God's perspective that is not an accurate diagnosis. Death doesn't always happen in an instant, but the death process can take place for a period of time before the actual physical death occurs. We should always remember that in the absence of love all creation begins to die.

Remember that 1 John 4:7, 8 says we are to love one another because love is of God and loving others is the distinguishing characteristic of being one of God's children. Our primary purpose in life is to impact everyone we meet with the love of God. Once we understand and begin fulfilling our purpose, the love in us will become nourishment for those around us. This will give us a renewed sense of purpose in life because we are doing exactly what we were created to do!

Everything God has created is interconnected. It is love that enables this to be true and our role is as important as ever. Just as the earth's vegetation emits the oxygen we breathe, as Believers we are responsible for saturating this earth's atmosphere with the love of God. As we become walking, talking, demonstrations of love, we become immune to the attacks of the enemy and increase our longevity!

Remember the Love Law

In Proverbs 3:1, 2, King Solomon says something we should keep close to our hearts, *"Forget not my law; but let thine heart keep my commandments: For length of days, and long life, and peace, shall they add unto thee."* Galatians 5:14 tells us exactly what this law is—love. All the covenant rights which give us access to a long, healthy, and prosperous life can only be accessed by walking in love. As we make the conscious effort to develop this love, it releases peace and abundant life.

It is imperative that we understand that the love of God in us is what enables us to obey what He tells us to do. Throughout the Word of God we see that adhering to God's commands brings life (Proverbs 4:4). The good news is that God doesn't command us to do anything He has not already equipped us to carry out. His love is the essential ingredient we need to reciprocate love to God and honor Him by obeying what He says in the Word.

The Benefits of Love

God doesn't give us instructions because He is trying to be mean or ruin our fun. On the contrary, He wants the very best for us. His instructions are not designed to be a hindrance or put a damper on our lives (1 John 5:3). A simple way to look at the benefits of love is: love = obedience = fulfillment of the commandments = experiencing the unlimited treasures of God's Word. This is the formula for long life.

In my quest to understand the benefits of living the "love-life" I discovered some interesting research that was published in "The Utah Statesman" by Jennifer Brennan, in regards to Valentine's Day:

> *"Love is in the air. Well, it is supposed to be on this special holiday. Whatever the case may be, research findings are showing love can be healthy."*

Glen Jenson, a Utah state University Family and Human Development professor and extension specialist says:

> *"People who feel loved, or when it's reciprocated, research says, live longer, happier*

lives, have better health, and make more money. Not only do people who feel loved have a better life expectancy, but when people experience relationships with other people, they often experience a healthy lifestyle...in the other aspect, people who do not experience that encouragement or love in their lives from others may be more prone to depression or loneliness."

There was another study performed at Yale University by Dean Ornish, M.D., that involved 119 men and 40 women who underwent a coronary angiography. Interestingly, those who felt the most loved and supported had substantially less blockage in their arteries than the other subjects.

A few years ago researchers at HeartMath used their tools to teach 30 people how to feel love in a conscious manner. One month later, they measured the study subjects' levels of both cortisol and DHEA, known as the anti-aging hormone. They found that the cortisol levels for the whole group had decreased 23 percent while the group's DHEA levels increased 100 percent across the board.

Clearly the evidence is overwhelming that love has a very real effect on our physical condition and quality of life. When we feel loved it releases chemicals called endorphins. Endorphins also stimulate other cells in our bodies that stimulate our immune system and improve our digestive system. The bottom line is, the love God has deposited in us, and entrusted us with, has a much greater purpose than what most people ever experience or demonstrate. It is the powerful, unlimited, and unmatched capability that is the essence of God Himself. When we love God and others the way Jesus commanded, we will be transformed from the inside out and our world will be impacted in an unprecedented way.

THE LOVE THAT LASTS FOREVER

"Love never fails [never fades out or becomes obsolete or comes to an end]…" (**1 Corinthians 13:8**, *The Amplified Bible*)

Some time ago the Lord charged me with imparting truth about the preeminence, value, and unlimited power of His love to the body of Christ. I remember asking the Lord to give me an in-depth understanding of His love, unlike what I had previously known. I wanted to be able to share the depth of it with those who would receive it so they would be enlightened, empowered, and restored in every area of their lives.

Although the manifestations of God's love are unlimited, we should pay particular attention to its ability to heal from the inside out and restore that which has been lost.

Most people seek love in one way or another without ever realizing the reason why they are so hungry for it. The reason is because we were created with a space inside us that only God can fill. His love is what makes us whole and complete. Knowing that love binds us together, builds genuine relationships, and ultimately makes life worth living. We crave love because God created us to give and receive it.

Different Types of Love

Many times people get confused about what love really is. There are different types of love that we must keep in perspective so we don't get off track in our relationships. Agapé love is the unconditional love that is the character of God. It is the highest type of love described in 1 Corinthians 13. It loves no matter what is done to it, or what our emotions are telling us. It is the opposite of carnal, natural love that is emotional, flighty, and easily moved by circumstances and situations. Natural love can also be based on feelings of lust or sexual desire.

The God-kind of love in us is the only love that truly satisfies for the long haul. It is the unyielding power and constant force that overrides anything we face in this physical realm. Agapé love is eternal. Not only does this love have longevity but it also has the ability to bear up under *anything*. When the love of God in us is fully developed, we can accomplish anything, be anything, and literally overcome the world.

Romans 5:5 says, *"And hope maketh not ashamed; because the love of God is shed abroad in our hearts by the Holy Ghost who has been given unto us."*

This simply means that when we became born again, a deposit was made on the inside of us that empowered us with the same ability that Jesus had to love unconditionally and have genuine, long-lasting relationships. Not only does this love have longevity but it also has a withstanding force that can bear up under anything.

A great example of this agapé love can be seen in the relationship between David and Jonathan in 2 Samuel 1:26. The love they shared as covenant friends exceeded natural standards.

Now in today's society, many would say this type of unconditional love is not possible; however, God's love is supernatural and differs greatly from natural, human love. God's love loves regardless of any circumstance and is ready to forgive any and all trespasses without passing judgment. Agapé love is willing to draw out and believe the best of every person.

Love's Healing Power

Matthew 22:39 instructs us to love our neighbor as we love ourselves. This is the second part of the Great Commandment. In reality you will never know how to love your neighbor until know how to love yourself. The relationships we have with others are a high priority to the Lord. This is an area where most of us are blowing it. We are to love others with the everlasting type of love that does not give up, cave in, and quit when things get difficult. This everlasting love increases our patience with one another and allows us to forgive that which is seems unforgivable. It is what enables us to love those we really don't like!

It is impossible to fulfill God's commandment to love if we try to accomplish it through our own ability; our emotional love is not enough to get the job done because it magnifies the faults of others rather than the good. It loves based on what it can get out of the deal, rather than looking to bless the other person. Natural love is selfish. However, the love of God is just the opposite. It doesn't base whether it will love on how it is treated.

One of the main reasons why some Believers have a difficult time having successful relationships is due to past hurts, pain, and abuse that they refuse to release to God. Consequently, it interferes with their present. However, the love we possess is the healing agent that each of us needs in order to be restored to wholeness.

Before we can heal the nations we must first heal one another. God's love fills in the gaps and replaces what we are lacking in our lives. It heals, overflows, and overwhelms any trespasses and transgressions we or others may have committed. It is the same love that enabled Jesus to forgive our sins and it gives us the ability to forgive those who have sinned against us as well.

Lust vs. Love

Please understand that lust and love are two different things altogether. Lust is selfish and always looks for ways to fulfill itself. It cares nothing about giving the advantage to others and will always cause people to compromise the Word of God. We can see this particularly where sex and relationships are concerned. When lust begins to chip away at our sense of morality, it doesn't value things like virginity and will always cause people to cross boundaries. Even the value and sanctity of marriage and genuine relationships become insignificant when viewed through a lens of lust.

Unlike the eternal quality of godly love, lust is temporary and lives in the moment. Not only that, but it is never satisfied. This is why individuals with sexual addictions can never get enough. Lust takes until nothing is left, whereas love gives on a continual basis.

Saints listen! The fulfillment of lust is a momentary thing, but can leave a lifetime of consequences in the aftermath. It causes spouses to walk out on their marriages, and it destroys relationships. Although unfortunate, it is statistically proven that the divorce rate is higher among Christians than unbelievers. But when we allow the love of God to rule our lives, the boundaries of relationships will be respected and marriages can weather the test of time.

Self-evaluation is necessary for growth in life. As we strive to make love our lifestyle, we should always take inventory of our own lives and look for areas where improvements can be made. I don't know about you, but I want my life to be an accurate reflection of God's character. I encourage you to meditate on the truth of God's eternal love, and look for ways to express that unconditional love to those around you. You may need to forgive someone, or release an offense perpetrated against you. As hard as it may be, recognize that when you mimic Jesus in your relationships, you please Him and demonstrate who He *really* is to the world.

WHAT DOES LOVE HAVE TO DO WITH MONEY?

"And though I bestow all my goods to feed the poor, and though I give my body to be burned, and have not charity, it profiteth me nothing." **(1 Corinthians 13:3)**

The principles of God's Word are like keys that open the doors to His blessings in our lives. Many times, these keys must be turned simultaneously, similar to a bank vault, in order for us to gain access to the treasures inside the vault.

A major area the body of Christ must master as it relates to activating spiritual principles, deals with the financial realm. God wants us to discover the direct connection between activating His love and financial prosperity. We must overcome the fear of running out in order to benefit from the fail-proof system God has designed for us to prosper. This system is known as "seed time and harvest."

God's divine system of increase has existed since the foundations of the world. The principle of the seed being able to produce a harvest can be found in Genesis 1:29,*"And God said, behold, I have given you every herb bearing seed, which is upon the face of all the earth, and every tree, in the which is the fruit of the tree yielding seed; to you it shall be for meat.*" What God was literally saying was, "I have not only given you the tree and the herb but also the *seed* within the herb." God not only gave provision, but He gave the source of the provision as well. As long as there is a seed, there will always be a harvest.

Seed time and harvest is a universal principle that will work for whoever will get involved. Genesis 8:22 says, "*While the earth remaineth, seedtime and harvest, and cold and heat, and summer and winter, and day and night shall not cease.*" This principle is as predictable as the seasons and the consistency of day and night! It will never stop working.

In order to activate and see the full benefits of seed time and harvest to our advantage, the condition of our hearts must be right. As this principle relates to our financial giving, the issue is not so much the amount of money we give, but the motive of the heart. If faith, love, and a desire to increase the Kingdom of God and be a blessing are our motives, our seed is guaranteed to produce an exponential harvest.

Many people wonder why they don't see any manifestation from their giving, but they do not realize that if the love of God, which purifies the heart, is not coupled with their seed, they won't see the results they desire. An excellent example is found in Mark 12:41-44 when Jesus was sitting at the treasury observing the attitude, or heart condition, of those who gave an offering. Surprisingly, He acknowledged the poor widow woman who gave only two mites. Although it was an extremely small amount, it was a huge offering in relation to what she possessed. Because she gave in faith, and with a pure heart, Jesus said she actually gave the most! Unfortunately, for many people, when it comes to giving their finances, they yield to fear rather than faith. The feeling of self-preservation that comes over us when it comes to giving is what stops our harvest.

Loving God vs. Loving Money

Money in and of itself is not bad; it is our relationship to it that can cause problems. We live in a world where the love of money is the standard and the constant pursuit of financial assets is the driving force. However, money is something God wants us to use to bless others. It is when our *love* for money and material possessions overrides our love for God and our desire to obey Him that we get into trouble.

Mark 10:17-22 recounts the story of the rich young ruler, a man who was seeking answers from Jesus about how to obtain the true riches of eternal life:

"And when he was gone forth into the way, there came one running, and kneeled to him and asked him, Good Master, what must I do to inherit eternal life? And Jesus said unto him, Why callest thou me good? there is none good but one, that is God. Thou knowest the commandments, Do not commit adultery, Do not kill, Do not steal, Do not bear false witness, Defraud not, Honour thy father and mother. And he answered and said unto him, Master all of these have I observed from my youth. Then Jesus beholding him loved him, and said unto him, One thing thou lackest: go thy way, sell whatsoever thou hast, and give to the poor, and thou shalt have treasure in heaven: and come and take up the cross, and follow me. And he was sad at that saying, and went away grieved: for he had great possessions."

I want to take note of a few things in this passage, one being that when Jesus replied, "One thing thou lackest;" His statement was followed by a colon, which is always used to describe or explain what was said before the colon. What Jesus was saying was, "It's great that you have been following the commandments but you lack one thing: let me show you what I mean."

When He instructed this young man to sell His possessions and follow Him, He was trying to position him for something greater than material wealth. He wanted him to realize that it does no good to follow the commandments of God while neglecting to operate in His love. The rich young ruler was religious, but when it came to obeying God from his heart, he failed the test. The love of God is what must motivate our giving, not religious routine. John 3:16 says God so loved the world that He *gave* His only begotten Son. If we truly love God, we will give Him anything He asks or requires of us, from our hearts.

Giving Expresses Love

God's love has the ability to purify our hearts, determine the measure of our giving, and add equity to our seed. The lesson of the rich ruler was that he didn't have the love of God backing up his actions, otherwise he would have been able to give bountifully without reservations. You see, the same love that compelled God to give His Son and the same love that moved Jesus to fulfill His assignment is the same love we possess in our hearts. We, too, can demonstrate our love for God through our giving. When the seed time and harvest principle is coupled with the love of God, profit is inevitable.

Giving is the byproduct of charity, which is the love of God. It is a tender-loving kindness that compels us to give. The word *charity*, translated in Greek, is the word *agapé*, which means benevolence, or an inbred type of affection which compels one to give. This is the heart of God.

The love of God that was deposited in us is the same love that compelled God to give so bountifully. First Corinthians 13:3 says, *"And though I bestow all my goods to feed the poor, and though I give my body to be burned, and have not charity, it profiteth me nothing."* The word, *bestow*, means to give, and giving activates the seed time and harvest process.

As it relates to our finances, we must begin to allow this type of love to govern our sowing. Second Corinthians 9:6 (*The Amplified Bible*) says:

> *"[Remember] this: he who sows sparingly and grudgingly will also reap sparingly and grudgingly, and he who sows generously [that blessings may come to someone] will also reap generously and with blessings. Let each one give as he has made up in his own mind and purposed in his heart, not reluctantly or sorrowfully or under compulsion, for God loves (he takes pleasure in, prizes above other things, and is unwilling to abandon or to do without) a*

*cheerful (joyous, "prompt to do it") giver [whose heart is in his giving]. And God is able to make of grace (every favor and earthly blessing) come to you in abundance, so that you may always and under all circumstances and whatever the need be self sufficient [possessing enough to require no aid or support and furnished for every good work and **charitable** donation]."*

This passage is so eye-opening because it shows us that God is clearly more concerned with the motive behind our giving than He is with the amount we sow. Now is the time to take inventory of our lives and evaluate whether we are giving money because it is a religious duty, or because we really desire to be a blessing to the Kingdom of God. Do we give because we love the Lord, or because we hope to get something from Him?

A great way to illustrate the heart-seed connection is to think about how pills are coated with a fructose compound that helps deliver the medicine to our internal systems in a more efficient manner. Similarly, the condition of our heart is what "coats" the seeds we sow in the Kingdom of God. When we want to truly please God in our financial giving, our harvest will be accelerated. When His love is the motivation behind our actions, we will begin to see results in our lives like never before.

THE BONDING EXPERIENCE

"From whom the whole body fitly joined together and compacted by that which every joint supplieth, according to the effectual working in the measure of every part, maketh increase of the body unto the edifying of itself in love." (Ephesians 4:16)

God is all about relationships! As we reflect on the commandments given to us by our heavenly Father it becomes apparent that they are categorized into three areas; our relationship with God, our relationship with ourselves, and our relationship with others. God works through relationships so it makes sense that how we treat and relate to one another is very important to Him. He cares about things like unity and harmony. The awesome part is that He has given us exactly what we need to bond with one another, and have meaningful, fulfilling relationships. This is His goal for the body of Christ.

Matthew 22:37 and Romans 5:5 are two familiar scriptures that communicate the importance of loving God and others. When we perfect our "vertical" relationship with the Father, our "horizontal" relationships with each other will thrive. Operating in love in our relationships will revolutionize the world because we will be compelled to have a greater level of respect for one another. If love became the governing standard as God originally intended, even things like violent crime would drastically decrease.

Love is a force that can change things for the better. It is also the distinguishing mark of the Christian because it is the inner energy that draws the unsaved world to the Lord. We have heard sayings like, "Love makes the world go 'round" and "What goes around comes around," and these clichés are actually true. Love does make the world go around because God, who is love, created this world in which we live. His love is the sustaining power of the universe. Not only that, but when you sow this love into the lives of others, you are guaranteed to receive it back.

Christians have a mandate in this world to build sound, wholesome, and loving relationships with one another. As we develop this love, we will find that our guards will come down and we will be less defensive. I even believe that racial, denominational, and cultural barriers will be eliminated when people get a taste of the God-kind of love.

The Main Ingredient

Only the love of God can truly unite us; it is the main ingredient that facilitates a true bond between people. If there is no love, there is no bond, and where there is no bond, a relationship will fail. Listen, the love of God in you has the ability to incite the love of God in someone else! Once both individuals begin to experience the benefits of love, their trust in each other will be established and complete honesty and transparency can take place.

Ephesians 4:15, 16 (*AMP*) says:

> *"Rather, let our lives, lovingly express truth [in all things, speaking truly, dealing truly, living truly]. Enfolded in love, let us grow up in every way and in all things into Him Who is the Head, [even] Christ (the Messiah, the Anointed One). For because of Him the whole body (the church, in all its various parts), closely joined and firmly knit together by the joints and the ligaments with which it is supplied, when each part [with power adapted to its need] is working properly [in all its functions], grows to full maturity, building itself up in love."*

This passage of Scripture clearly shows us how the love of God is unlimited and has many functions, the primary one being facilitating unity between people. It is by God's design that His love in us is what compels us to develop a healthy bond with others. The body of Christ can never truly unite without allowing the love of God to draw us closer to each other.

Natural Evidence

From a natural perspective, there is even a physiological love connection that takes place in relationships. In the May 1st issue of *Biological Psychiatry* (http://www.elsevier.com/locate/biopsychiat), published by Elsevier, several researchers began a study on the effects of Oxytocin, also known as the "love hormone." This hormone is produced in the hypothalamus region of our brains and is responsible for the bonding that takes place after mating, as well as the bonding that takes place between a mother and child immediately following birth. It also helps to forge trust between humans.

These scientists conducted an experiment on several adult couples who ingested Oxytocin prior to having a "conflict discussion." Some of the couples received a placebo and the findings were quite interesting. It was concluded that the love hormone increased positive communication behavior between the couples who were exposed to it.

Apparently, Oxytocin sends chemicals throughout the body in a way that causes us to lower our defenses. When our shields are down, trust is extended and true heartfelt relationship can be established.

The research results presented here give further evidence that love has a bonding effect, even on a physiological level. God's love in us has the ultimate objective of allowing us to experience the highest level of human interaction. When we yield to it, our lives will never be the same.

LOVE THEM TO LIFE

"For if ye love them which love you, what reward have ye?" (Matthew 5:46)

One of the most important responsibilities we have as Believers is to win unbelievers to Christ through the witness of our lives. We must be on fire for the Lord! In order for us to fulfill our mission we must be consistent and passionate about the things of God. This fervency is generated by our love for God and the unconditional love we have for one another. Many times we fail to reach people because we are either too aggressive or not persistent enough. However, when we employ the love of God, it ensures the proper balance and the right approach.

The love on the inside of a Believer is like a lighter that ignites a flame. Once lit, this flame produces an attractive light that is undeniable to the world. This light serves as the identifying mark of the Christian, which points those who do not know the Lord to Jesus Christ. The measure of love operating in you determines the intensity of your light.

When you look at the word *light* you will find it has many synonyms including fire, flame, electricity, and illumination. Matthew 5:14-16 describes Christians as being the "light of the world" and that we are to be on display as a signpost pointing people to Jesus Christ. The Lord didn't give us His light for no reason! He gave it to us so we can provide light to those who don't have it, and so that our Father will be consistently glorified.

There are too many Christians wallowing in depression, living in fear, and walking around hopeless. All these negative emotions are designed to subdue the light of God. And if we, who are the light bearers, allow our light to be subdued, those in the dark will never see the Way who is Jesus! Our light plays a critical role in God's plan to reach the lost, all over the world!

Keep in mind that in order to have light it must be generated from a main source. The Word of God says that God is the source of all power and that He is love. Therefore, *love* is the source of all power. If we trace our light to its origin, we will find the love of God yet again.

Seeing Through the Love Lens

As we begin to cultivate this love, it will heighten our concern for others and awareness for their welfare. It will empower us to be compassionate toward those who do not know Jesus, allowing us to look beyond their conduct and compelling us to love them to life!

Ephesians 2:11, 12 remind us that all of us were without Christ at one point so we are in no position to scrutinize another's sin. However, it is the love of God in us which enables us to see things from God's perspective.

Many Christians envy unbelievers who are wealthy or seem to have a measure of success in life. However, as long as a Christian feels inferior to an unbeliever they will not be compelled to even address the issue of salvation with them. Seeing the world this way doesn't line up with God's vision for our lives. We should always remember that even though a person possesses great material wealth, if they do not know the Lord they are on a fast track to destruction. The love of God in us should compel us to want to reach out to those who are lost, regardless of how successful they may appear to be.

When an unsaved person comes in contact with a Christian, the love in us should quicken that individual to life on some level. They should leave your presence feeling affected in some way, shape, or form.

Love is particularly effective in overcoming offense. Matthew 5:43-48 instructs us to love our enemies, bless those who curse us, do good to those who hate us, and pray for our persecutors and abusers. When we do this, we demonstrate we are truly children of God. We exemplify the Kingdom of God when we act like Jesus.

As difficult as it is, seeing through the lens of love is necessary for our spiritual development and also for drawing others to the Lord. To demonstrate agapé love in a world that prizes the "eye for an eye" mentality is not the norm. However, by allowing our love light to shine, the more people will want to know about the God we serve. Let's love them to life!

GROWING IN LOVE

"And above all things put on charity, which is the bond of perfectness."(Colossians 3:14)

There is a difference between growth and development. For example, a person's physical body will automatically grow until they reach a certain age, but if that individual wants to develop a more muscular physique, they will have to exercise and apply pressure to stimulate that type of development. The same thing is true in the life of a Christian. In order to develop in certain areas of our lives, we must make the effort on our part. God wants us to move out of the baby stage of Christianity and into maturity. The true test of that maturity is the degree to which we walk in love. When we develop in the things of God, it positions us to receive His best in our lives.

Please understand that maturity is not automatically determined by a person's chronological age. Let me explain; someone could be chronologically 40 years old, and have an appearance that is consistent with their age, however, when it comes to their spiritual and emotional I.Q. they may be on the level of a 16 year old or younger. Many times people who have experienced some sort of negative or traumatic experience earlier in their lives become emotionally frozen at the age where the incident occurred. This is why many times some adults tend to handle situations from a child's perspective.

Fortunately, with life comes experience that forces us to grow and change. I am sure you have heard someone say, "If I knew then what I know now, things would be a lot different." As we mature spiritually, we see, hear, and understand things better.

In my personal life there are several situations that I would love to be able to "do over." But imagine if our level of maturity enabled us to have the discernment to make the right decisions from the beginning? Maturity heightens our senses, allowing us to see trouble before it comes our way. When we develop in God's love, we position ourselves to live discerning lives and remain protected. Love is what gives us this supernatural ability.

Desire Love above All

Many Christians want to operate in the gifts of the Spirit, which is wonderful. However, none of the gifts work properly without the foundation of love intact. First Corinthians 12:31 says we should desire and cultivate spiritual gifts; there is nothing wrong with that. But it also says the most excellent and highest virtue of all is love. When love is perfected in our lives, we have come that much closer to achieving spiritual maturity. This is even more important than all the wonderful works we do for God's Kingdom.

When you study out the word *perfect*, it actually translates into "maturity." It doesn't indicate being flawless, without spot or blemish, but it does define an elevated sense of knowledge that comes by way of maturity. First Corinthians 13:10-13 says:

> *"But when that which is perfect is come, then that which is in part shall be done away. When I was a child, I spake as a child, I understood as a child, I thought as a child: but when I became a man, I put away childish things. For now we see through a glass, darkly; but then face to face: now I know in part; but then shall I know even as also I am known. And now abideth faith, hope, charity, these three; but the greatest of these is charity."*

We have to grab hold of what the Apostle Paul is saying here. When we mature spiritually, we leave our old ways and mindsets behind in favor of the higher ways and godly mindsets. When perfected love becomes the standard of our lives, our understanding of God's ways of doing things will be enlightened.

First Corinthians 14:1 says we should *eagerly pursue* and seek to acquire love. The Apostle Paul distinctly separates love from spiritual gifts, however. Love is not a gift, it is a necessity. He says to make it our greatest aim above all other things, including our gifts, because it is the power that enables the gifts to operate properly.

A true test of spiritual maturity is our ability to love those who seem to be unlovable. Matthew 5:43-48 (*AMP*) says:

> *"You have heard that it was said, You shall love your neighbor and hate your enemy; But I tell you, Love your enemies and pray for those who persecute you, To show that you are the children of your Father Who is in heaven; for He makes His sun rise on the wicked and on the good, and makes the rain fall upon the upright and the wrongdoers [alike]. For if you love those who love you, what reward can you have? Do not even the tax collectors do that? And if you greet only your brethren, what more than others are you doing? Do not even the Gentiles (the heathen) do that? You, therefore, must be perfect [growing into complete maturity of godliness in mind and character, having reached the proper height of virtue and integrity], as your heavenly Father is perfect."*

The love of God in us is what determines our level of maturity and provides evidence that we are the sons and daughters of the most High God. This love is the evidence our godly pedigree and distinguishes us from everyone else. Once it is cultivated, it enables us to exceed the limitations and boundaries of natural love in order to accomplish what is ordinarily hard on our flesh.

Have you wondered why some Christians can bless others with their mouths but turn around and curse them out if they do something that offends them? Quite simply it is because they haven't cultivated the love of God to the point of having a heightened awareness of how to treat others. Natural love will never enable us to go the extra mile when someone hurts us. Godly love on the other hand helps us develop into full maturity.

Exercise Love

In order to develop something, it has to be used regularly, or exercised. The same is true with love. If we want to grow in this area, we must look for opportunities that challenge our flesh and force us to choose between love and selfishness. When we are on the quest to cultivate love, the enemy will make sure we have plenty of opportunities to work our "love muscle." It is during those times that we must refer back to God's Word and adopt the proper response.

Remember that natural, human, carnal love will never enable us to fully mature or compel us to go the extra mile in our relationships with others. Only the supernatural love of God gives us the ability to love those who are unlovable and forgive those who have hurt us. As difficult as it may be, following Jesus' example will pay off in the long run. It is to our advantage to commit to becoming more like Him in our character and responses.

Why is growing in love so important for the Believer? Well, because it puts us in the perfect position to receive the fullness of our inheritance. Galatians 4:1-7 discusses the fact that as long as an heir is a child, he is no different than a slave, and has no access to the inheritance that belongs to him. However, when that child grows up and become mature, he has a right to fully partake of his inheritance. Every promise of God hinges on His love, and our ability to receive. Make a decision to grow in love so you can be a fully developed member of the body of Christ. Then you will be able to manifest the true nature of God to all those with whom you come in contact.

WE ARE ONE RACE

"There is neither Jew nor Greek, there is neither bond nor free, there is neither male nor female: for ye are all one in Christ Jesus." (Galatians 3:28)

In today's society it is clear that there is more division than ever before. So many differences keep us separated from one another, not only physically but in our hearts as well. Things like denomination, ethnic background, and economic status keep us from truly being able to love each other the way God intended. If we are to ever move into the fullness of our purpose as the body of Christ, these barriers must be broken.

Division can be caused by a strong dislike, a deep hatred, or prejudice which is birthed out of ignorance. Consequently, we remain confined to our personal world, afraid of reaching out to those who are different from us. The Word of God says that in the last days the love of many would wax cold, meaning that even Christians would begin to repress the love God put in their hearts, and instead be selfish and fearful. Unfortunately, when love is absent, everything else begins to deteriorate.

God's love is designed to transcend barriers and it enables us to love one another beyond the superficial level. Agapé love unites people regardless of skin color or ethnic background.

From one Race Came Many Ethnicities

The idea of "race" is actually not accurate from a biblical standpoint. When God created Adam and Eve, there was no distinction of their ethnic background. Unfortunately, our society is consumed with race and color complexes. However, God's love is intended to reunite people so we no longer see one another by the pigment of our skin, but by the condition of the heart. We are all part of one race called the *human* race.

In order to gain a better understanding of this whole issue of color and race, we need to go back to the beginning in order to annihilate a gross misconception dealing with skin color.

First, God created Adam and Eve with the same color. Eve came out of Adam and was a reflection of him in female form. This is why Adam was able to say, "This is now the bone of my bone and the flesh of my flesh." Considering that Adam and Eve had the same skin color, it would be highly unlikely that those who descended from them looked any different. In fact I believe God did not create a "black," "yellow,"or "white" race. Instead, in His divine wisdom He designed our bodies with something called melanin because he anticipated mankind being scattered to the four corners of the earth during the building of the Tower of Babel.

The Gene Factor

In an interesting article by Jamie Conklin, of Stanford University, she addresses the question, "Where do different skin colors come from?"

In her article she explains:

> "*Human skin color can vary from almost translucent to almost black. This range of colors comes from the amount and type of a pigment called melanin found in the skin.*
>
> *There are two types of melanin—eumelanin and pheomelanin. In general, the more eumelanin in your skin, the darker your skin will be. People who make more pheomelanin than eumelanin tend to have lighter skin with freckles.*
>
> *Like many other traits, the amount and kind of pigment in your skin is controlled by genes. The version you have of each of these genes work together to create the final product—your skin color.*

To understand how this issue of how skin color works, we'll talk about some of the genes that scientists have found that affect human coloring. We will also look at how vitamins and where your ancestors lived might have played a role in determining your skin color.

Melanin and Your Skin

Melanin is made in special cells called melanocytes. These cells are found in the epidermis of your skin. There are at least three ways people can end up with different skin color: 1) if your skin produces less pigment, which results in lighter skin color, 2) having fewer melanocytes, or 3) the kind of pigment your skin produces.

There are two types of melanin; eumelanin, which produces black or brown pigment, and pheomelanin, which is red or yellow pigment.

People who make lots of pheomelanin tend to have lighter skin, often because of freckling, which takes place when melanocytes clump together.

Melanocytes are usually spread evenly in the skin so when freckles form, some spots of the skin have lots of melanocytes (freckles) and other spots have few or none. Where there are no melanocytes, the skin is very fair.

Skin Color Genes

Scientists have figured out that several genes are involved in skin color, one of which is the melanocortin 1 receptor (MC1R). When MC1R is working well, it causes melanocytes to convert pheomelanin into eumelanin. If it is not working well, then pheomelanin builds up.

Most people with red hair and/or very fair skin have versions of the MC1R gene that don't work well. This means they end up with a lot of pheomelanin, which leads to lighter skin.

Two other skin color genes were first identified in fish. One gene was found in stickleback fish and the other in zebrafish. Researchers studying the stickleback fish found that the kit ligand gene (kitlg) was different between dark and light stickleback fish. They also found that humans have different versions of this gene as well and that certain versions lead to lighter skin.

The kit ligand gene is needed for the survival of melanocytes. So if a person (or a fish) has a version of this gene that doesn't work well, their melanocytes won't survive as well. Fewer melanocytes will mean less pigment and lighter skin.

Researchers studying zebrafish with light colored stripes found another gene involved in human skin color, SLC24A5. The fish with light colored stripes had a version of this gene that didn't work well. When they researched the gene in people, researchers found that some lighter skinned people also had a poorly working version of this gene.

Unlike the case with kitlg, scientists don't know for sure what SLC24A5 does. Some clues suggest that it may be important for moving calcium into cells. It may be that calcium is important for having more melanin in cells.

Scientists have figured out that lighter skinned East Asians get their skin color mostly from a non-working version of kitlg. Northern European people with lighter skin often have a poorly working version of SLC24A5. A small number of pale northern Europeans get their skin color from a non-working MC1R gene.

Although these three genes help to account for skin color differences between populations, there are probably other genes that scientists have yet to find. And scientists are hard at work to find the genes that make different people within a population have different colored skin.

Why different skin colors may have evolved

It is pretty obvious that people whose ancestors come from Northern Europe or Japan tend to have lighter skin than people whose ancestors are from sub-Saharan Africa or Australia. The reason for these differences may have to do with the amount of sunlight in each place.

Sunlight can be pretty dangerous because of its ultraviolet (UV) light. UV light can destroy folic acid or cause changes (mutations) in the DNA of some skin cells. Sometimes, these mutations can lead to skin cancer.

Not surprisingly, darker skin is helpful when there is a lot of sunlight. But sunlight isn't all bad. It can help our bodies make vitamin D, which is a vital nutrient. When we don't have enough Vitamin D, it can cause problems with our bones and a deficiency has even been linked to some types of cancer.

When our skin gets UV rays from the sun, our bodies use the UV light to make Vitamin D. But melanin in our skin acts like a filter, making it harder for people with more melanin (darker skin) to make vitamin D. This means that the more melanin you have, the more sunshine you need to make enough vitamin D.

Imagine if you lived somewhere cold and dark. Your skin wouldn't see much sunshine. How would your body get enough sunshine to make all the vitamin D you needed? Well, if your skin had less melanin (which would make it lighter colored), then you would need less time in the sun to make enough vitamin D!

With all this said, it is quite possible that lighter skin evolved so that people in darker places were able to get all of the vitamin D they needed to stay healthy. So the skin color you have might be a result of how much sun your ancestors got.

We can now clearly see that skin color is just a matter of how much melanin you have. The versions of the skin color genes tell your body how much melanin to make. All of this means that the difference between dark and light skin is only a few changes in DNA."

Information adapted from the article "Ask a Geneticist." Jamie Conklin, Stanford University

What Really Matters

What is more important than the ethnicity of Adam and Eve is that they were part of the human race of people. They were God's perfect creation. Perhaps that is why the Bible puts more emphasis on how God made man in His image than it does on describing all the physical characteristics of these two people. What we do know about them is that their spirits were infused with God's love.

The truth is no matter what color our skin is, if we were to cut it, we would all bleed red. Listen, the separation of race is something conceived out of ignorance and was never God's intention. From God's perspective there is no such thing as a black man or a white man. He sees mankind as a reflection of Himself, regardless of skin color.

And while we were all created uniquely for a reason, from a spiritual perspective there are really only two groups of people: those who are part of the Kingdom of God and those who are not. In the Kingdom of God, skin color, ethnicity, culture, and economic status mean nothing.

Clearly, we have been blindsided by the devil for years in this area. In his attempt to keep us from coming together as one unrelenting force in the earth, he has used superficial differences to keep us separated from each other. Language, culture, and personality differences have all been characteristics that have caused division. Color in particular has been the major source of contention, but this should not be our focus as children of God.

Matthew 22:39 commands us to love our neighbor as we do ourselves. This commandment is intended to bridge the gap between people of different colors, denominations, and cultural backgrounds and get us to look beyond ourselves and see the bigger picture. It is intended to unite a nation that has been deceived into thinking that we are unequal.

The division of color has killed millions, ruined countless lives, and destroyed many families. However, the moment we grab hold of the fact that we are not distinguished by our outward physical characteristics, the more effective we will be for the Kingdom.

Division based on superficial qualities has done much damage in the body of Christ. However we each have a responsibility to walk in love toward *all* people and see them through spiritual eyes rather than through the eyes of prejudice.

Unity is the Key

Psalm 133:1-3 says something powerful:

> *"BEHOLD, HOW good and pleasant it is for brethren to dwell together in unity! It is like precious ointment upon the head that ran down upon the beard even Aaron's beard: that went down to the skirts of his garments; as the dew of Hermon, and as the dew that descended upon the mountains of Zion: for there the Lord*

commanded the blessings, even life forever more."

It has always been God's desire for mankind to dwell on Earth in peace and unity. The reason is that when we are all on one accord, it places a demand on the power of God; there is power in agreement!

The only way to counteract the spirit of division is the love of God. Each of us must make a commitment to renew our minds as it relates to how we view other people and determine to see them the way God does. When our level of spiritual maturity rises above the ignorance that has permeated our society, it will enable us to see one another as a significant part in God's divine plan.

Do You See What I See?

I see a multitude of people from all walks of life; that have united in one faith, willing to end all strife.

They have come to the conclusion that we have always been related, now instead of hate, it is love that is demonstrated.

They no longer magnify differences in one another because the way they love themselves, they also love their brother.

The denominational barriers are finally hewn down, like the walls of Jericho they have been reduced to the ground.

One language, one speech, and one vision in mind, let us make a name for the Lord and let our light shine.

The light is so intense, like a city set on a hill, drawing sinners from the dark and fulfilling God's will.

There is one sovereign God who created you and me; I stop to pose the question, "Do you see what I see?"

Jeffrey Glover

RETURN UNTO ME

"If my people, which are called by my name, shall humble themselves, and pray, and seek my face, and turn from their wicked ways; then will I hear from heaven, and will forgive their sin, and will heal their land." **(2 Chronicles 7:14)**

The last few decades have seen a massive explosion of technology that is undeniable. The Internet has become a major form of communication and digital capabilities are ever expanding. I believe God is definitely on the move and is using such media outlets to spread the Gospel message. However, Christians must be mindful to not become so caught up in the information highway and the trappings of the world that they lose sight of building proper relationships and remaining focused on God in the midst of it all.

Prior to preparing a sermon for my congregation, I always ask the Lord what is in His heart that He would like to share with His people. I must say, it is truly disturbing to hear the grief in His heart as He shares His concerns. The truth is many of us have been seduced and deceived by the world, and it is affecting our relationship with the Lord.

It is necessary for us to keep in mind that everything we need and desire belongs to God; all things were created by and for Him. Regardless of who currently possesses the resources of the earth, they ultimately belong to the Father. Therefore, we do not have to strive to achieve these things. When we know who we are in Him, we already have access to them! All we must do is position ourselves by faith to receive.

In the Garden of Eden, when God asked Adam where he was after he had sinned, it wasn't because God didn't know! He wanted Adam to recognize and acknowledge the place from which he had fallen.

Adam represented humanity at that time, and yet there are still many people whom God is asking the same question. In order for man to return to God we must first realize that we have turned away from Him.

Deuteronomy 8:11-20 contains instructions from God to not turn away from His commandments:

> *"Beware that thou forget not the Lord thy God, in not keeping His commandments, and His judgments, and His statutes, which I command thee this day. Lest when thou hast eaten and are full, and hast built goodly houses, and dwelt therein. And thy herds and thy flock multiply and thy silver and thy gold is multiplied, and all that thou hast is multiplied; then thine heart be lifted up, and thou forget the Lord thy God,*

which brought thee forth out of the land of Egypt, from the house of bondage; who led thee through the great and terrible wilderness, wherein were fiery serpents, and scorpions, and drought, where there was no water; who brought thee forth water out of a rock of flint; who fed thee in the wilderness with manna, which thy fathers knew not, that he might humble thee, and that he might prove thee, to do thee good at thy latter end; and though say in thine heart, my power and the might of mine hand hath gotten me this wealth. But thou shalt remember the Lord thy God: for it is he that giveth thee power to get the wealth, that he may establish his covenant which He sware unto thy fathers, as it is this day."

It is amazing how certain mindsets can survive thousands of years and extend from one generation to the next. Once the Israelites were delivered from captivity and were blessed with substance, their vision became clouded and their hearts turned away from the Lord. Romans 11:11, 12 says, *"I say then have they stumbled that they should fall? God forbid: but rather through their fall salvation has come unto the Gentiles, for to provoke them to jealousy. Now if the fall of them be the riches of the world, and the diminishing of them the riches of the Gentiles; how much more their fullness?"*

We have to understand what happened here. God originally initiated a covenant with the children of Israel in which He provided all they could ever need and more than they could possibly desire. However, they rebelled against God and turned away from Him. As a result, God offered the covenant blessings to the Gentiles, or those who are not Jewish.

Because of our sinful nature prior to receiving Christ, we involuntarily followed the same lustful and rebellious trend as the Israelites did. Even to this present day, most people have forsaken God. Many of the recent events that have transpired in our economy are no coincidence. When we begin to take prayer and reverence for God out of schools and the justice system it affects the nation, even to the point of financial collapse.

Even the family unit, particularly in America, has been mesmerized by the fringe benefits of the covenant while inadvertently forsaking it at the same time. One of the reasons why God chose Abraham is because He knew Abraham would teach God's covenant to his children and that his children's children would keep the covenant. Somewhere along the line we have lost sight of the significance of the relationship God has offered us. We must get back to honoring this relationship in order for things to turn around.

By doing a simple assessment of our daily routines, we can determine where we are specifically as it relates to our relationship with God and whether He is our priority. Do we spend time with Him in prayer and in His Word? What about our finances and relationships? Is love the governing force and motive for what we do, how we think, and what we say to others? We must take inventory of ourselves, locate where we are, and make the necessary adjustments to correct any areas that have gotten out of alignment.

Staying Focused

As we move closer to the Lord's return, there will continue to be an increase in idolatry and people turning away from God in record numbers. However, the body of Christ must guard against the lust and attraction of the world. To love Him requires total commitment and focus. When we love God completely, there is no room for distraction.

Sometimes we can find ourselves doing all the ministry-related things church requires, but our hearts are still out of alignment with God. Revelations 2:3, 4 admonishes us to not abandon our first love—God—even in the midst of our serving Him. Our primary objective must be maintaining a thriving relationship with Him at all costs.

Keep in mind that blessings are always birthed out of intimacy with the Lord. In this world there will always be daily opportunities to become distracted through the cares of the world and the lust of other things. Staying focused requires deliberate intention to keep our eyes on Jesus! Anything we exalt or acknowledge more than the Lord will end up taking His place and becoming our god. When this happens, the curse of lack can enter into our lives.

Matthew 6:19-24 gives some very valuable advice for the Christian:

> *"Lay not up for yourselves treasures upon earth where moth and rust doth corrupt, and where thieves break through and steal: but lay up for yourselves treasures in heaven, where neither moth nor rust doth corrupt and where thieves do not break through nor steal: For where your treasure is, there will your heart be also. The light of the body is the eye: if therefore thine eye be single, thy whole body shall be full of light. But if thine eye be evil, thy whole body shall be full of darkness. If therefore the light that is in thee be darkness, how great is that darkness! No man can serve two masters: for either he will hate the one, and love the other; or else he will hold to the one, and despise the other. Ye cannot serve God and mammon."*

We must shift our focus from what we can accumulate in this world and keep our attention on the source of all things—God. Our worth is not determined by the assets we acquire on this earth. Essentially God is saying that if our primary focus is on the creation, it will take our focus off the Creator. Whatever it is that you treasure in your heart will be the object of your attention.

Notice in this passage of Scripture, he says the light of the body is the eye. The light he is speaking about in this chapter is directly related to the light he spoke about in the previous chapter when he said, *"ye are the light of the world."* In the current chapter he provides insight on what determines the intensity of our light. Depending on what enters through your eye gates determines the light or darkness in your soul. If we fail to guard what enters into our hearts through our five senses it will create a gross darkness that will provide us with just enough pleasure to keep us out of God's presence.

Submitting to God

God desires so very much for His people to return to Him and it happens when we humble ourselves and submit to His Word. James 4:7-10 in The Amplified Bible says:

"So be subject to God. Resist the devil [stand firm against him], and he will flee from you. Come close to God and He will come close to you. [Recognize that you are] sinners, get your soiled hands clean; [realize that you have been disloyal] wavering individuals with divided interest, and purify your hearts [of spiritual adultery]. [As you draw near to God] be deeply penitent and grieve, even weep [over your disloyalty]. Let your laughter be turned to grief and your mirth to dejected and heartfelt shame [for your sins].   Humble yourselves [feeling very insignificant] in the presence of the Lord, and He will exalt you [He will lift you up and make your lives significant]."

James says a mouthful in this passage that literally provides the answers to re-establishing a relationship with our heavenly Father. As you read this passage carefully you see James says, *"As you submit yourselves to God it will enable you to resist the devil."* The more we submit to God the greater resistance we have against the devil! He goes on to say the devil will flee, or run in terror and be repelled, because the Spirit of God that is in you has now come *on* you as a reward of your intimacy.

A distanced relationship with God is what causes disloyalty, wavering, and divided interests. As long as we are content in that state we will always be alienated from God's promises. Although earlier in this chapter I mentioned the peril of America; the separation between God and mankind is a worldwide problem that has eroded the very foundations of society.

In his instructions, James used two words of great significance: *submit* and *humble*. It requires a humble heart to submit, or surrender, to God when we have thought and conditioned ourselves for ages that we are our own source and there is no God. We literally have to die to our flesh and selfish ways in order to live life for God! Anything He requires of us is always for our ultimate good.

I am sure we can all admit to the negative impact that taking prayer out of schools has had in the school systems both at home and abroad. I had the privilege of enjoying my earlier school years in Copenhagen, Denmark where the Bible was an actual curriculum; but ever since God became unimportant to mankind, we have witnessed a severe moral decline.

In so many places in the Word of God it is written, *"Return unto me..."* Returning to God is the prerequisite for us to regain His image. As we regain His image we regain our dominion, power, and authority in Him. John 14:6 says, *"Jesus saith unto him, I am the way, the truth, and the life: no man cometh to the*

Father but by me." Whenever we lose sight of Him, who is the Way, it is inevitable that we will lose *our* way!

I like what Isaiah 44:22 says, *"I have blotted out, as a thick cloud, thy transgressions, and, as a cloud, thy sins: return unto me; for I have redeemed thee."* The Lord paid the ransom for us to be able to have an intimate relationship with Him, so for us to return unto Him is our reasonable service. You see, in order to *return* there had to be an initial turn away from Him. In other words something lured, enticed, and drew our attention away from God to such a point our backs were turned to him. We moved from a position of reverence and worship to neglecting our relationship with Him!

Deuteronomy 30:8-10 (AMP) gives wonderful insight into the benefits of returning to God and honoring Him:

> *"And you shall return and obey the voice of the Lord and do all His commandments which I command you today. And the Lord your God will make you abundantly prosperous in every work of your hand, in the fruit of your body, of your cattle, of your land, for good; for the Lord will again delight in prospering you, as He took delight in your fathers, If you obey the voice of the Lord your God, to keep His commandments*

*and His statutes which are written in this Book
of the Law, and if you turn to the Lord your
God with all your [mind and] heart and with all
your being."*

This return to God must take place not only on a
personal level but on a national one as well. It is time
to put prayer back in schools and acknowledge godly
principles as the foundation of our country. Returning
to God will enable us to reclaim our original identities
and walk in the power and authority we have been
given.

There are many more scriptures that carry rewarding
promises associated with returning to the Lord. He is
always standing at the door of our hearts, knocking
and awaiting our response. Can we hear Him? When
we choose to open the door, we will see what real life
is all about. God's love hasn't gone anywhere. On the
contrary, love is waiting with open arms for us to
return and experience the fullness of all He has
planned for our lives. Now is the time to repent and
return. Will you answer the call?

Conclusion

More than anything, God wants His people to walk in love toward one another. Honoring Him isn't just about all the religious things we do in church; it is about the love walk, first toward Him and then toward those with whom we come in contact. In addition, we must learn how to love ourselves unconditionally because in order for us to effectively love our neighbor, we must first love ourselves. Until we establish a well-balanced, godly relationship with ourselves, we will not have the wholeness that compels us to love others the way we are commanded by God.

Friend, the same love that moved God to reach out to us and forgive us is the same love we inherited to extend to one another. The love of God compels us to see and treat one another as God sees and treats us. The Word of God says, *"By this love all will know that we are His disciples indeed."* The word *indeed* in today's terms means "sure enough," "most definitely," and "beyond a shadow of a doubt!" The love of God in you compels you to walk in a level of discipline that reminds people to whom you belong.

I want to encourage you to judge your heart and look at your life. Is there anyone toward whom you are holding bitterness or unforgiveness? Are you carrying hurts and wounds from your past that you need to release to God? Don't allow anything anyone has done to you to hinder you from the blessings that come through walking in love. The price Jesus paid for us to have a relationship with the Father was too great; He requires us to treat others the way He did—with unconditional love, compassion, grace, and forgiveness.

You have the power to execute the very same actions and character that Jesus did during His earthly ministry. Every day, make a commitment to allow your life to be governed by the love of God. Repent and return to Him if you have allowed other things to take His place. He is waiting to receive you with open arms. It is through your expression of God's character that the world will know who you belong to and whose Kingdom of which you are a part. Allow your life to be governed by love!